Getting t
on Time

by Linda Kita-Bradley

Grass Roots Press

Acknowledgements

Grass Roots Press acknowledges the financial support of the Government of Canada for our publishing activities.

Canadä

Produced with the assistance of the Government of Alberta through the Alberta Multimedia Development Fund.

Albertan

Editor: Dr. Pat Campbell
Photography: Susan Rogers
Book design: Lara Minja, Lime Design Inc.

Library and Archives Canada Cataloguing in Publication

Kita-Bradley, Linda, 1958–, author
        Getting to work on time / Linda Kita-Bradley.

(Soft skills at work)
ISBN 978-1-77153-221-1 (softcover)

        1. Readers for new literates. 2. Readers—Punctuality.
3. Readers—Time management. I. Title.

PE1126.N43K582558 2018   428.6'2   C2017-906935-7

Part 1

Leo and Cora are friends.

They work at a diner.

Leo is always on time.

Cora is always late.

Today, the dishes pile up.

Leo works fast.

But he can't keep up.

The pots and pans pile up, too.

Cora is still at home.

What should she wear?

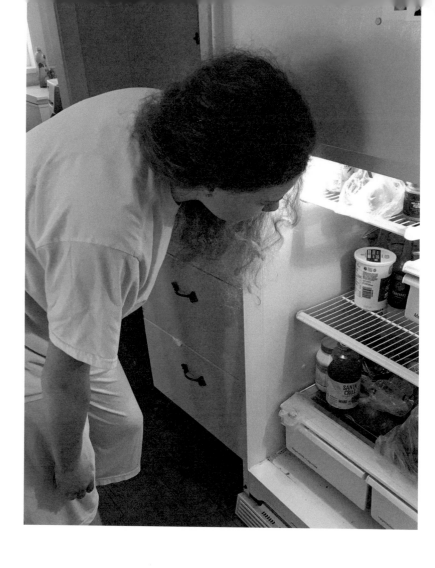

What should she make for lunch?

Where are the keys?

The next day, Cora sleeps in.

She looks at the clock.
Late again!

At work, the dishes pile up again.

Leo is not happy.

The next day, Cora is late again.

Cora's mom wants to talk.

Cora listens.

Cora finally gets to work.

Leo is mad.
He will not speak to her.

Cora says, "I thought we were friends."

Talking About the Story

1. Imagine you are Cora.
   Why are you always late?

2. Imagine you are Leo.
   What do you want to tell Cora?

3. Do you know someone
   who is always late?

   How does being late
   affect co-workers?

Part 2

Read the next story about
Cora and Leo.

How is it different from
the first story?

Leo and Cora are friends.

They work at a diner.

Leo is always on time.

Cora is always late.

Leo is not happy.

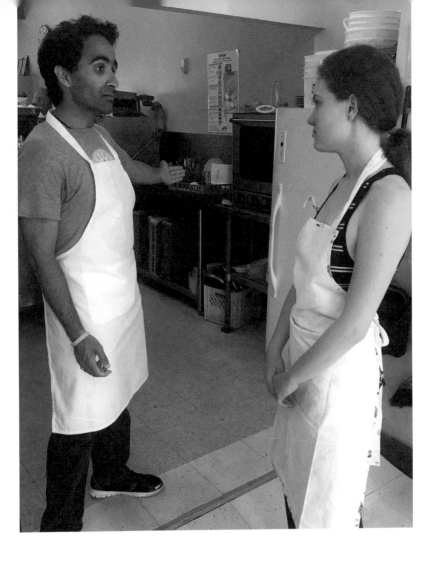

So Leo talks to Cora.

He says, "I need you to be on time."

"The dishes pile up fast."

"I can't keep up."

That night, Cora makes her lunch.

She puts her keys on the table.

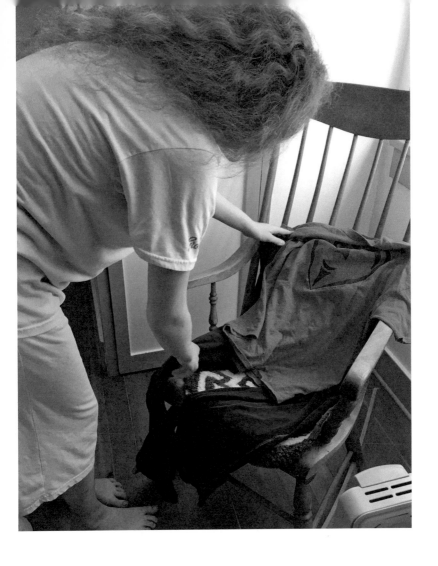

Cora lays out her clothes.

She goes to bed early.

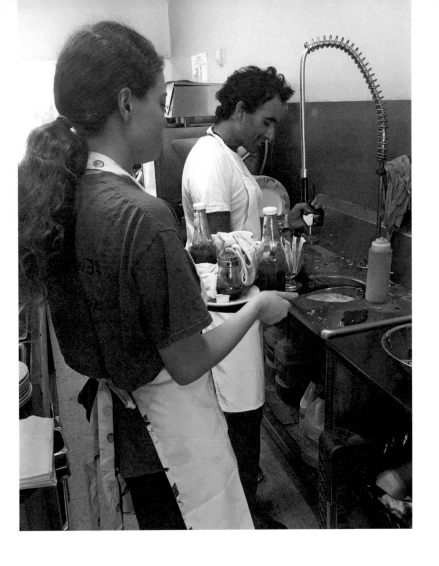

The next day, Cora is on time.

The next week, Cora's mom
is very sick.

Cora phones Leo.
She says, "I will be late."

Cora takes her mom to the doctor.

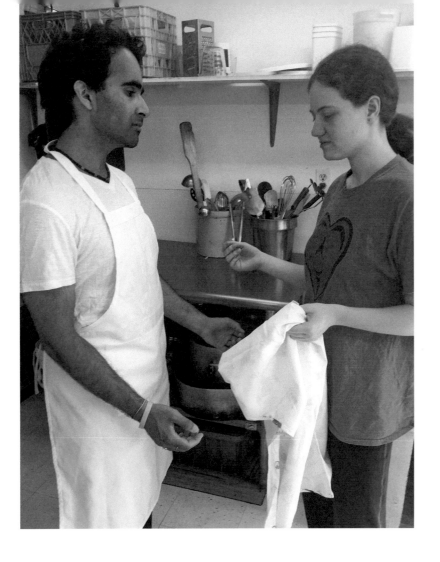

Cora finally gets to work.

Leo gives her a hug.

Cora says, "My mom is okay."

Cora and Leo start to work.

Made in the USA
Columbia, SC
13 September 2024

42020056R00029